D1263059

RACIAL PROFILING AND DISCRIMINATION

YOUR LEGAL RIGHTS

CORINNE GRINAPOL

ROSEN PUBLISHING

New York

Published in 2016 by The Rosen Publishing Group, Inc.

29 East 21st Street, New York, NY 10010

Copyright © 2016 by The Rosen Publishing Group, Inc.

First Edition

Expert Reviewer: Lindsay A. Lewis, Esq.

Library of Congress Cataloging-in-Publication Data

Grinapol, Corinne, author.
Racial profiling and discrimination: your legal rights/Corinne Grinapol.
    pages cm.—(Know Your Rights)
Includes bibliographical references and index.
ISBN 978-1-4777-8020-6 (library bound)—
ISBN 978-1-4777-8619-2 (pbk.)—
ISBN 978-1-4777-8620-8 (6-pack)
1. Race discrimination—Law and legislation—United States—Juvenile literature. 2. Minorities—Legal status, laws, etc—United States—Juvenile literature. 3. Narcotic laws—United States—Juvenile literature. 4. Juvenile justice, Administration of—United States—Juvenile literature. 5. Racial profiling in law enforcement—United States—Juvenile literature. I. Title.
KF4755.G75 2016
363.2'308900973—dc23

2014040242

Manufactured in the United States of America

CONTENTS

INTRODUCTION

I n a video interview, Anthony, a high school student in Chicago, describes his first run-in with the police. He was leaving a party at 10:30 PM and stopped at a corner. A police car pulled up, and the police inside called him over. Anthony recalled the cops in the car saying, "Get him! Get him." Anthony got scared and ran. Multiple cars and police with dogs chased him, catching up with Anthony at a gas station. The police tackled Anthony to the ground and handcuffed him. With Anthony sitting in the back of a police car, the officer checked his background to find he had a clean record.

When they discovered his record was clean, they brought him home. His dad asked the cops why his son had been handcuffed. They said it was a case of mistaken identity—Anthony looked like a gang member they were on the lookout for.

The party Anthony had left when the cops stopped him? It was an eighth-grade graduation party. Anthony recalled another detail about the party. When he left the party, he had walked out with another kid, a boy who was white. Anthony was black. The two had walked out together, but Anthony was the only one who had been picked out by the police to be stopped. Since that day, Anthony has been on guard when he walks on the streets, afraid he will get stopped by cops for no reason other than walking while black.

Stories like Anthony's are far from rare. At every point in the system, from school suspension to sentencing and incarceration, minority youth are targeted for punishment at rates much higher than those for white youth.

In many cities and towns across the United States, your racial and ethnic background could affect your interactions with the police.

This resource will help you understand the inequalities that exist in the criminal justice system and how those inequalities can affect your life. It will also help you to become aware of those rights that you have and will help you come up with strategies to avoid getting caught up in that system.

If you are already in trouble, if you are facing suspension or expulsion from school, if you find yourself in detention waiting to come up in front of a judge, don't lose hope. Know there are people and organizations out there that exist to help navigate the system, fight for freedom, and help defend your rights. This resource will help you figure out how to get those people to fight for you.

CHAPTER 1

THE SCHOOL-TO-PRISON PIPELINE

Although the best way to avoid jail is to stay in school, the popularity of certain new policies and trends has made this harder than you think. These rules not only make it harder for children to stay in school, but push kids straight out of school and into the criminal justice system. This phenomenon is known as the school-to-prison pipeline.

One policy making this possible is zero tolerance rules, where one mistake can lead to a suspension—no

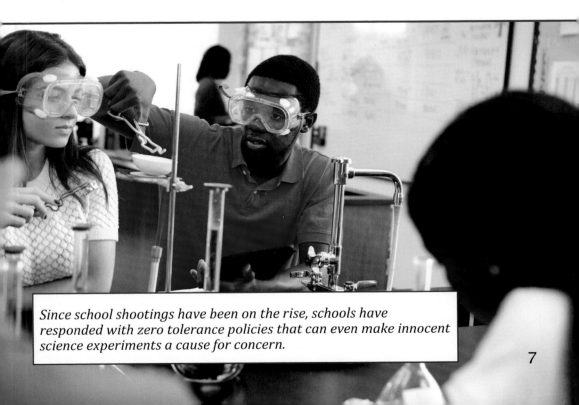

Since school shootings have been on the rise, schools have responded with zero tolerance policies that can even make innocent science experiments a cause for concern.

questions asked, no exceptions. This happened to Kiera Wilmot, a student at Bartow High School in Florida. She brought part of a science experiment with her to school for her teacher to approve: toilet bowl cleaner and aluminum foil mixed in a plastic bottle. She was planning to make a volcano and was told by a friend this would make the volcano explode. When her friends convinced Kiera to show them the experiment in the schoolyard, things went horribly wrong. Smoke poured out of the bottle, and there was a small explosion. An assistant principal saw what happened, and Kiera explained that she had no idea that would occur. In the school's opinion, it didn't matter that it was an accident, no one got hurt, and no property was damaged or that Kiera was a good student who had never been in trouble. The school saw Kiera's bottle as an explosive. She was taken out of the school in handcuffs, and the assistant attorney decided to charge her as an adult on two felony counts, including possessing a weapon. Fortunately, the charges against Kiera were dropped. Kiera was expelled and sent to an alternative school, however, where she felt the material was a lot less challenging than what she was used to.

Many times students of color like Kiera are viewed as less innocent than white students. A cycle of profiling, arrests, and images in the news and media help keep this cycle going. Fortunately for Kiera, her story has a happy ending. A NASA astronaut who saw her story raised money for Kiera to continue to explore her love of science by sending Kiera and her sister to space camp.

Another change has made being arrested in school a frightening reality for a growing number of children. Although schools would traditionally hire private security

When police officers replace security guards in schools, the number of school-based arrests tends to rise, making this an area of concern for those trying to end the school-to-prison pipeline.

guards to look over safety, a growing number of schools and districts are now hiring police officers. Just like on the streets, and unlike security guards, these officers have the power to arrest kids in school. Things that used to get you sent to the principal's office—getting into a fight, yelling at your teacher—can now get you in handcuffs.

THE UGLY TRUTH OF ZERO TOLERANCE

According to the U.S. Department of Education, during the 2011–2012 school year, 36 percent of students across the country who were expelled were white. Thirty-four percent were black. The numbers seem even, but a little more than half the population of students is white, whereas just 16 percent is black. So the likelihood of a black student getting expelled is much higher than that of a white student. And it isn't just expulsion rates that are uneven. The differences start in preschool, where 48 percent of students who have been suspended more than once are black, compared to just 26 percent of white students.

Overall, a black student is three times as likely to be suspended or expelled than a white student. And while boys make up 79 percent of all suspensions, the percentage of black girls who are suspended, 12 percent, is double the percentage of all white boys who are suspended.

According to the U.S. Department of Education Office for Civil Rights, students with disabilities are twice as likely to get suspended as students without disabilities. "American Indian and Native Alaskan students are also disproportionately suspended and expelled, representing less than 1% of the student population but

2% of out-of-school suspensions and 3% of expulsions," a big number for such a small population.

Although these numbers make up the average for states as a whole, some states are even more unequal in the rates that black students are suspended compared

Even missing a few days of school can make a huge difference academically. A suspension can make catching up seem like an impossible task.

GET YOUR STORY OUT THERE

In a ninth-grade biology class at Olive Branch High School in Mississippi, students stood in front of their science projects as the teacher took photos of each group. When the teacher took a photo of Dontadrian Bruce and his group, Dontadrian posed with his thumb, pointer, and middle fingers raised. It was a number three, the number he wore on his jersey when he played football for the school's team. The school administration, when they saw the photo, interpreted it entirely differently. The assistant principal accused Dontadrian of belonging to a gang. Three days later Dontadrian was called up before a disciplinary panel. They had found a photo of gang members making the same symbol Dontadrian had made. This was the evidence they pointed to when they told Dontadrian he was suspended and that they were recommending he be expelled from the school. That photo was the only evidence they had. They didn't look at his grades, which were all As and Bs. They didn't talk to his coach, who said he would have been shocked if Dontadrian belonged to a gang and that it was highly unlikely given how intense football practice was.

It could have ended there, another story of a kid suspended and forced to leave school on flimsy proof of belonging to a gang. However, Dontadrian's mother, Janet Hightower, decided to do everything in her power to get Dontadrian back in school. She relentlessly worked for justice. She told the American Civil Liberties Union (ACLU) and the local chapter of the National Association for the Advancement of Colored People (NAACP) about his situation. Now she had two influential civil rights organizations working on her case.

Just as important, she told the media. Hightower contacted news organizations and told her son's story. Soon Dontadrian's case was on NBC News. Dontadrian and his family were interviewed by their local ABC News station and told their side of the story on television. As the story exploded in the news and on social media, his high school got a lot of attention. Three weeks later, the school told Dontadrian he could come back. His mother made sure Dontadrian's return to school came with no strings attached, such as the original plan to let him back but with probation.

Dontadrian's story shows that there are effective ways to fight back when you feel you have been treated unjustly. Look for organizations in your area, such as the NAACP and the ACLU, that exist to protect the rights of citizens like you. Believe that your story is important and look for ways to tell it. Local news stations and newspapers have websites with tip lines and contact information that allow you to call or e-mail them to let them know about your situation. Don't give up.

to white students. The states with the biggest disparities are Arkansas; Washington, D.C.; Illinois; Michigan; Missouri; Nebraska; Ohio; Pennsylvania; Tennessee; and Wisconsin.

The justification for using zero tolerance policies to suspend, expel, or send students to jail is that they make schools safer. The policy became more popular around the time of the April 1999 school shooting in Columbine, Colorado. Many administrators saw those policies as a way to prevent similar horrible situations from happening. However, research shows that this isn't the case. School is the safest place for kids to be.

What's more, kids who are suspended are either kept away from school completely or, like Kiera, sent to

Knowing your school's and district's rules will help you be prepared to fight back when you feel you have been treated unfairly.

disciplinary alternative schools. Although suspension is jokingly called a "vacation" from school, all those days of lost teaching make it harder to catch up when students return. It can be so hard that they end up dropping out, which dramatically increases their chances of getting arrested for a crime. Those who get pushed out of school and never finish are much more likely to end up in the criminal justice system.

KNOWLEDGE IS POWER

Statistics show that students of color have the odds stacked against them. Chances are their behavior will be noticed and scrutinized more closely than white students' behavior. This is highly unfair, and there is a movement out there seeking to change this. In the meantime, don't give up. You must be the protector of your own rights. And the first step to protecting your rights is knowing what they are.

Be aware of school and district conduct and discipline policies. Even if your school never explained the rules to its students, not knowing the rules isn't an acceptable excuse when you are accused of breaking them. Be proactive. If you aren't told what the rules are, seek them out. Check your school and your district website for a copy of the code of conduct. If one isn't available online, ask a teacher, principal, or assistant principal.

Once you have a copy, read it. You will learn what your school and district considers permissible behavior, what isn't allowed, what the punishment for breaking the rules could be, and what the disciplinary process

SO YOU'VE BEEN SUSPENDED

If you've been called out for breaking a rule and brought to the principal's office, it's your chance to explain your side of the story. Even if you're fuming inside, stay cool. Calmly and respectfully tell your story. Even if you feel you've been called out unfairly, yelling or displaying anger will not help. If you know the rules and don't believe you have broken them, explain this, using the code as your proof.

Sometimes even the best defense doesn't work. But suspension isn't a reason to give up. First read through the code of conduct for information about suspensions and the suspension process. Check with your district and state to see if they have additional information on suspensions that isn't in the code of conduct. You have rules to follow. So does your school. Make sure your school is following the process exactly as it is supposed to. Make sure your school provides you with all the required information about your suspension. If you find the school isn't following proper procedure, make a physical note of what it has failed to do, being as specific as possible.

Make sure you know the reasons the school has suspended you and the type of suspension you are facing. The suspension policies will explain what you can do to challenge the suspension, such as bringing in your parent or guardian for a meeting with the principal or filling out an appeal, or official challenge, to your suspension. If you make an appeal or challenge your suspension, the observations you wrote about how your school wasn't acting properly will help your case. Your school may not be required to tell you that you have those rights, which is why it is so important to find out about them on your own.

If you face an expulsion, you might want to think about getting a lawyer to fight for you. Some organizations offer free legal aid to kids. Check the back of this resource for organizations to contact. If you have already been suspended, these organizations can help you figure out what your next steps and options are, such as asking for your suspension to be overturned, or fighting your suspension outside of school, like in court.

could and should look like. Knowing the rules will help keep you from breaking rules you didn't know existed. If you are accused of breaking the rules, knowing the code will help you figure out if the accusation is just. It will help you know if the discipline process you find yourself going through or the punishment you may be receiving is what you should be getting, according to the code. It's a lot harder to take away the rights of someone who is prepared to protect them.

CHAPTER 2

RACIAL PROFILING

P olice make decisions all the time about who to stop, question, and investigate. When the decision to investigate someone is based on their race, religion, ethnicity, or the country they are originally from, this is an unfair discriminatory practice known as racial profiling. Racial profiling takes many forms in this country. Following are a few real-life examples.

Profiling is a common practice in many airports across the country. Certain ethnic groups are stopped at higher rates than others.

On September 11, 2011, Shoshana Hebshi was sitting in an airplane waiting for it to take off when policemen boarded the plane and stopped in her aisle. They put her and the two Indian American men seated next to her in handcuffs and took them all off the plane. The policemen wouldn't tell Hebshi why she was being arrested, and she was strip-searched and held for four hours before being let go. Hebshi, who has one Jewish and one Arab parent, filed a lawsuit with the ACLU claiming she was racially profiled. The ACLU later found out that the reason Hebshi was arrested was because she was sitting next to the two Indian American men who were reported to be "acting suspiciously" and because of her Arabic last name.

The U.S. Department of Justice (DOJ) did a study on Alamance County in North Carolina. They discovered that Latino drivers are ten times more likely than any other group to be stopped while driving and two times more likely to be arrested during a traffic stop. Because of the study, the DOJ has a lawsuit against the county's sheriff, Terry Johnson, accusing him of racial profiling. Witnesses claim the reason so many Latinos were arrested is because the sheriff was looking for undocumented immigrants to kick out of the country. The sheriff could only check on the immigration status of people who were arrested. This is the reason many believe so many more Latinos were stopped.

Eric Holder, an African American who served as the attorney general and the head of the U.S. Department of Justice during the Obama presidency, talked about his own experience with racial profiling. While walking to the movies in a wealthy neighborhood in Washington, D.C., Holder and his cousin were stopped by police for no apparent reason. Even though he was working as a prosecutor at that point, the color of his skin still made him a target.

STOP-AND-FRISK

The most infamous use of stop-and-frisk is in New York City, where police officers have used this tactic for over a decade. The stop-and-frisk policy allows a police officer to stop and hold a person on the street to question the person, as well as search, or "frisk" them. Police need a reason to stop a person. However, many of the reasons that police stop someone are so vague anyone can fit the bill. Members of the New York City Police Department (NYPD) will stop-and-frisk people if they look suspicious, make "furtive" movements, or are in an area that has a lot of crime. This last reason is especially questionable, because the U.S. Supreme Court decided it's unconstitutional to stop a person just because they are in a high-crime area.

The reasons police use to make stops are far from the only unusual things about stop-and-frisk. Minorities make up the overwhelming majority of people who are stopped and frisked. In 2002, the first year that the Center for Constitutional Rights (CCR) analyzed the stop-and-frisk data reported by the NYPD, there were 97,296 people stopped. Of the people stopped, 82 percent were innocent of any wrongdoing. Despite the fact that most people stopped were innocent, the amount of people stopped and frisked year after year kept going up. It reached a high point in 2011, when a total of 685,724 people were stopped. Of those, 88 percent were found to be innocent. That year

53 percent of people stopped—more than half—were black. Thirty-four percent were Latino. Just 9 percent were white. This wasn't unusual. Year after year, blacks and Latinos received the brunt of police attention for stops.

In interviews the CCR conducted with minorities who had been stopped, people described feeling humiliated and under attack. A teenage girl described how she and a group of her siblings and cousins, ranging in age from eight to sixteen, were stopped in the stairwell of their building; told to take off their socks, shoes, and hoodies; and were checked for drugs. Other people described how they no longer felt safe, how they felt they could be stopped by police at any point during normal activities: walking their street, sitting in the park, standing in front of their apartment building.

The victims of stop-and-frisk were not the only ones who felt they were being treated unfairly. Working with CCR, the victims of stop-and-frisk sued the police department and New York City in 2008, saying that the policy was unconstitutional and relied on racial profiling. The case was known as *Floyd vs. City of New York*. In 2013, the judge hearing the case agreed, saying that the NYPD's use of stop-and-frisk was unconstitutional. This did not, however, settle the matter. New York City appealed the judge's decision, and she was taken off the case. On August 6, 2014, the city withdrew its appeal, meaning that the city wasn't going to argue with the original decision. There was some damage done by the fact that the judge was removed from the case. Had her decision not been challenged in this way, people who wanted to argue against policies like stop and frisk in other states could have used her decision to strengthen their cases.

BROKEN WINDOWS

The idea behind broken windows policing is that small crimes lead to big crimes. If a window is broken in a neighborhood and nothing is done to stop it, soon people will think that no one cares and will break all the other windows. According to the theory, if police show that they're interested in maintaining "public order" or making sure everyone plays by the rules, then criminals will think twice about committing crimes. The idea behind broken windows policing was the work of two professors, George L. Kelling and James Q. Wilson, who in 1982 cowrote the article "Broken Windows," which was published in the *Atlantic Monthly.*

In July of 2014, Eric Garner, a black man, helped break up a fight on Staten Island. When the police got there, however, they tried to arrest Garner for selling "loosies," or single cigarettes. As Garner argued with police about the reason he was being arrested, the police put him in a chokehold and pushed him to the ground. Although Garner complained he couldn't breathe, they kept him in that position and he died on the street to the horror of everyone watching, all for the suspicion of selling some cigarettes.

Arresting or ticketing people for selling loose cigarettes is an example of broken windows policing. Here are some other things police go after under this policy: riding a bicycle on the sidewalk, walking through a park after dark, drinking on the street, not having a dog license for your dog, playing music too loudly, littering, spitting on the sidewalk, sitting on the steps of an abandoned house, and, yes, breaking a window.

Even though the idea of broken windows policing has been around for more than thirty years, there is still a debate about whether or not it works.

At first, the broken windows policy seemed to be working. As cities put broken windows policies in place, crime began to decline in those cities. However, crime also decreased in other cities that didn't use broken windows, places like Washington, D.C., which decided to have its police officers get to know the people in its communities better.

The consequences of broken windows may do a lot more harm than good. When someone pleads guilty to an offense like spitting on the sidewalk, it can go on his or her criminal record. Having a criminal record makes it harder to get a job, no matter the reason. That person may then end up doing something criminal to make money. What's more, broken windows, like so many of

Under broken windows policing, a quick nap on a park bench can get you a ticket or worse from the police.

SOCIAL MEDIA CAN SAVE YOUR LIFE

When the situation between Eric Garner and the police began to escalate, Garner's friend Ramsey Orta used his phone to record what was happening. Unfortunately, that video did not save Eric Garner's life. The video was shared on social media, however, and helped spread Garner's story. It made others care and brought attention to the story.

Recording a confrontation with the police, whether by taking video or photographs on a phone or tweeting or writing on Facebook in real time about what is happening, is an important tool. A video is evidence. If your story contradicts what the police say a video recording may shed some light on and back up your story.

Recording a run-in with the police can help your or someone else's case. Organizations like the ACLU have even created apps, like Stop and Frisk Watch, for this purpose.

A video can also help you fight for a larger issue. When teenager Alvin was stopped by cops in Harlem, he secretly set up his cellphone to record the stop. The video showed the cops pushing Alvin to the ground, calling him a mutt, and telling him they were going to beat him up.

Alvin's video was published on the *Nation* magazine's website. Soon, the city council was debating stop-and-frisk. When a judge ruled that New York's stop-and-frisk was unconstitutional, she mentioned the video in her decision.

You can use video and social media to protect yourself and to be an ally for others. If you see someone in a situation that doesn't look right, record or write down what you see. If you maintain an appropriate distance and are in a public space, it is within your rights to record police activity.

the other policies discussed, targets minorities more than whites. In New York City, 81 percent of the 7.3 million people ticketed from 2001–2013 were black or Hispanic. Sometimes there are deadly consequences, as we saw with the tragic case of Eric Garner.

If you get a ticket or summons under broken windows, what you do next is extremely important. First, go to court on the date shown on your summons. If you skip court, a bench warrant can be issued for your arrest,

Appearing before a judge can be an overwhelming experience. That's why it's important to know what to expect and to have people, like a lawyer, assist you with the process.

thus increasing the seriousness of the charges against you. If you do end up skipping a court date, it is best to be proactive about it and go to court as soon as you can to deal with the summons. Otherwise, you can be arrested if you are stopped and the officer checks your records. When you get to court, check to see if you have a right to a lawyer. A lot of times the judge or hearing officer will give you the option of pleading guilty and paying a fine instead of taking your case to trial. Be

careful of this. Even though you may avoid jail, a guilty plea will give you a criminal record. This will make it harder to get a job and may prevent you from getting government services or things like financial aid for college or could compromise your ability to join the army. A lawyer can help you make a decision about what to do and explain how your decision will affect your future plans, such as whether you want to work for law enforcement or go to graduate or professional school.

"AM I FREE TO GO?"

Being stopped by police when doing nothing wrong, especially in the context of racial profiling, is a situation that can produce a lot of stress and anger. However, being able to get through this incident as quickly and safely as possible requires the ability to put that anger aside. In this situation, anger, even if justified, can put the police on guard and cause the scene to worsen quickly.

Remember that although you don't have control over being stopped, you do have control over how you respond. Keep your emotions and language in check. Don't yell and don't talk back. In fact, don't speak at all. The right to remain silent is one of your most basic rights. It might seem unfair that you can't express how you feel, but the bigger goal is getting through a stop as quickly as possible.

Don't struggle with the police or try to resist. If you do, they can charge you with resisting arrest, even if there was no reason to stop you in the first place. Calmly make it clear, however, that you don't agree or give them permission for their search.

The exceptions to the do-not-talk rule include three phrases. The first is, "Am I free to go?" If they answer no, that means they are holding you. You have the right to know why, so your next question would be, "Why am I being detained?"

If the police begin to search you, don't struggle against it, but make it clear you don't agree to it by saying, "I do not consent to a search." If you are carrying a bag, don't open the bag for the police. Opening the bag for the police means that you are allowing them to search you, even if you haven't said this out loud.

Police must have a good reason to search you. This is called probable cause. If you allow them to search you, they no longer need probable cause. However, if you don't give them permission to search you and they find something on you, such as drugs or a weapon, they will have to prove in court that they have probable cause to search you, and racial profiling doesn't fit the bill for probable cause.

CHAPTER 3

DRUGS LAWS ARE NOT CREATED EQUALLY

In 1980, the rates at which young blacks and whites were arrested for drugs were about even. By the end of the decade, blacks were five times as likely to be arrested for drugs as whites. What had happened to cause this change? The War on Drugs.

The War on Drugs started back in 1971. The early focus was not on putting people in jail, but on helping people stop using drugs. Crack cocaine, which became a big problem in the '80s, would change this.

Crack is a type of cocaine that is smoked instead of snorted. Crack became particularly popular in poor, minority neighborhoods because it was cheap. It is also extremely addictive, and the costs of keeping up the addiction are high. The crack epidemic hit communities in an extremely destructive way. Addicts would get high in front of their kids, lose their jobs and friends, and sometimes lose their lives. Many women turned to prostitution to make enough money to keep buying drugs. As for the drug dealers, they handled competition for sales by building up gangs and getting into gun battles.

People were scared by what was happening in their communities. They wanted help. They wanted drugs out of their neighborhoods. In the 1980s, the government responded by stepping up the War on Drugs. Unfortunately, instead of focusing on helping people fight their addictions, the government focused on putting the problem away—literally, in jail.

The Anti-Drug Abuse Act of 1986 was a law that put money toward fixing the drug problem. It also created something known as mandatory minimum sentencing. Under mandatory minimum sentencing, if a person was caught with a specific amount of a drug, that person would have to go to jail for at least a certain amount of years—no exceptions. This type of sentence was meant to be a deterrent, or something that warns people away from doing something.

As it would turn out, there was a huge problem with this policy. Mandatory minimum went into effect when a person was caught with a certain amount of a drug. Being caught with one kilogram of heroin (about two pounds) or five kilograms of powder cocaine (about eleven pounds) led to a minimum ten-year jail sentence. Being caught with just five grams of crack, however, led to a minimum five-year sentence. To put this in context, five kilos is equal to five thousand grams.

Drug use and drug addiction was treated as a crime, rather than a terrible addiction. Because it took a dramatically smaller amount of crack to get a jail sentence, and crack was a bigger problem in poor minority communities, people began to connect the idea of drug use with the poor. Poor minorities became linked, an association that continues to have huge consequences.

MARIJUANA: THE NEW FRONT ON THE WAR ON DRUGS

Although large amounts of crack arrests and convictions continued in the 1990s and early 2000s, a new threat to the War on Drugs has emerged in the past decade and a half: marijuana. Between 2001 and 2010, there were eight million arrests related to marijuana possession or distribution, although the majority of those were for possession, according to an ACLU study of Bureau of Justice statistics. Marijuana-related arrests include a little more than half of all drug arrests. In fact, during that period, more people were arrested for marijuana than violent crimes.

With marijuana arrests, just like in so many areas of the criminal justice system, minorities pay a heavier price. Surveys on drug use, which ask people to answer questions about their drug habits, show that about as many black people use drugs as do white people. This rate is true for marijuana as well. You would expect that if drug use is even, arrest rates would be as well. But this is not the case.

Laws against marijuana are loosening across the country. In 2012, Washington and Colorado became the first states to legalize marijuana for nonmedical purposes.

THE REAL DEAL: RESULTS OF A DRUG CONVICTION

Marisa Garcia was driving with a friend near Los Angeles one day in 2000. She was about to turn nineteen years old and in a month would be going to her first semester of college at Cal State Fullerton. Garcia stopped for gas and left the car to pay. When she returned, Garcia discovered police searching the car. They found a small coin purse. Inside the purse was a pipe with some ash in it, according to Garcia. After police asked who the pipe belonged to and Garcia said it was hers, the police arrested Garcia and gave her a summons to appear in court.

Garcia decided to deal with this on her own, without telling her parents or getting a lawyer. When Garcia went to court, she pleaded guilty to marijuana possession and paid a $400 dollar fine. She thought her ordeal was over.

However, two months later, she learned that she had lost her federal financial aid for college. When you fill out a federal financial aid form, you are required to say whether or not you have ever had a drug conviction. Because Garcia had pleaded guilty, she had a drug conviction on her record. As a result, she lost her financial aid for a year.

Garcia thought she was going to have to drop out of school. Fortunately, Garcia's mother found a way to pay for that first year of college.

Having a drug conviction on your record can have serious consequences. It can keep you from getting federal money to help pay for college, as happened to Garcia. It can prevent you from being able to get public housing. When you apply for jobs, you are often required to say whether you have been convicted of a crime, and a lot of businesses will not hire someone with a record. If you are arrested for a crime and already have a drug conviction on your record, you may face a higher penalty if convicted. If you are faced with the issue of how to answer questions on a job or school application and have any doubt whatsoever as to what you should answer and how, you should consult a criminal attorney.

The stakes for immigrants or undocumented or permanent residents who are legally allowed to be in this country may be even higher. Although in California it is legal to carry less than 1 ounce (28 g) of marijuana, someone who the police think may be an undocumented immigrant who is found with less than an ounce of marijuana can be sent to an immigration detention center.

When you apply for federal financial aid for college, you must report any drug convictions. A conviction could mean the loss of aid.

Even a permanent resident, that is, someone who has a green card and is allowed by the government to be in this country, may risk losing that status and being deported, or sent back, to their original country if he or she has a drug conviction on his or her record. In fact, almost every drug conviction, except for possession of a small amount of marijuana, can get a permanent resident deported.

Even though it may seem a simple thing to plead guilty, pay a fine, and go on with your life, the costs of having a drug conviction on your record can follow you for a long time.

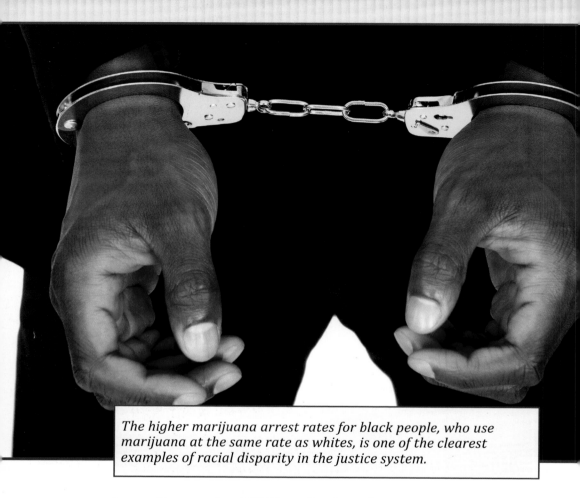

The higher marijuana arrest rates for black people, who use marijuana at the same rate as whites, is one of the clearest examples of racial disparity in the justice system.

According to the ACLU study, data from 2010 shows that out of every 100,000 black people, 716 were arrested for a marijuana-related drug offense. Out of every 100,000 white people, 192 were arrested. This means the chances of a black person being arrested for marijuana is 3.73 times higher than the chances of a white person. Since 2001, the difference in arrest rates between blacks and whites has grown bigger, not smaller.

What's more, the ACLU study showed that a black person is more likely to be arrested for marijuana than a white person in most scenarios: every state, in the city or the country, in a rich area or a poor area, in an area were blacks are a small part of the population, and in areas where blacks are a large part of the population.

Some states are worse than others. In Iowa, a black person is 8.34 times more likely to be arrested than a white person. In Washington, D.C., it is 8.05. In Pennsylvania, the seventh highest state for difference in rates, it is 5.19. The breakdown for counties doesn't always match the state breakdown. In Missouri, for example, a black person is 2.63 times more likely to be arrested, but in St. Louis County in Missouri, the rate for a black person is 18.4 times higher than that for a white person.

Young people are particularly vulnerable targets for marijuana arrests. In 2010, 62 percent of marijuana possession arrests were of people twenty-four years old or younger, while 34 percent were of people in their teens and younger.

What about other groups? The data for arrests comes from the FBI's Uniform Crime Reports (UCR). Like the census, Latinos aren't tracked separately, but are usually put in the white or Caucasian category. Because of this, it is hard to figure out marijuana arrest rates for Latinos. There are, however, a few states that do track arrests specifically for Latinos. In New York, for example, one of the few states that does have this information, Latinos are 2.5 times more likely to be arrested for marijuana possession than whites.

THE ROLE OF RACIAL PROFILING

Looking at the data on the differences in drug arrest rates between blacks and whites, a natural question appears: What is the cause of these differences? Racial profiling has a lot to do with it. In the decade that marijuana arrests kept climbing, so did another number: the amount of minorities stopped under programs like stop and frisk. Because more minorities come into contact with police through stop-and-frisk programs or traffic stops than do white people, the chances of police finding marijuana on them are higher. Even if, for example, there are just as many white people walking down the street carring a joint as are black people, the fact that they are less likely to be stopped and searched in general means there is less of a chance an officer will catch them with pot. Sometimes this happens over and over.

Alfredo Carrasquillo was first arrested for marijuana possession when he was fourteen years old and sent to juvenile detention. That was the first time he was charged with marijuana possession, but not the last. He now works as a community organizer and has tips about how to avoid being stopped, like wearing button-down shirts, carrying identification, and not standing on corners. The tips don't always work. Recently, Carrasquillo was hanging out with some friends on the grounds of a housing project when police officers told them to put their hands on their heads. The officers began searching through Carrasquillo's pockets and found a small bag of marijuana. He was arrested, sent to jail for three days, and strip-searched before his case was heard. He plead guilty and was charged a $120 fine. Carrasquillo's story is all too typical, and many teenagers have their lives changed in an instant if they are targeted for a stop when carrying marijuana.

Sometimes the effects an arrest and conviction will have on the rest of your life don't become obvious until much later.

CHAPTER 4

JUVENILE INJUSTICE

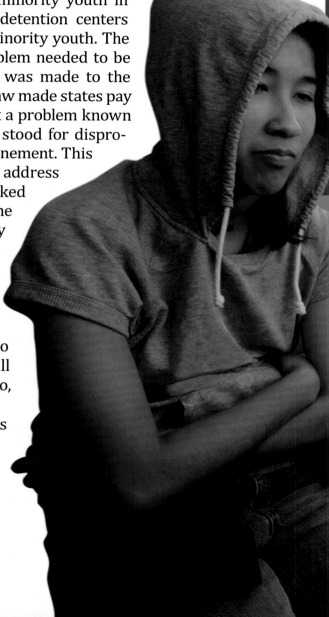

By 1988 it had become very clear that there were more minority youth in jails and juvenile detention centers than there were white minority youth. The government felt this problem needed to be fixed, so an amendment was made to the juvenile justice law. The law made states pay attention to and try to fix a problem known as DMC. Originally, DMC stood for disproportionate minority confinement. This meant it was supposed to address those youth who were locked up. The law compared the percentage of a minority group that was locked up to the percentage of a minority group within that state. If, for example, 14 percent of a state was comprised of Latino youth, but 30 percent of all youth in jail were Latino, this was a case of DMC.

In 1992 the law was changed again. DMC was changed to disproportionate minority

Everyone loses when teens are jailed. For the state, it's a loss of money better spent trying to improve the lives of teens at risk.

contact, and states were to fix not just the disproportionate amount of minorities who were locked up, but also the disproportionate amount of minorities having any kind of run-ins with the judicial system. The points of contact, which happen at every level of the juvenile justice system, are as follows:

> **Arrest:** An arrest is when law enforcement apprehends a youth for committing a crime.

> **Referral:** This is when the youth goes from arrest to processing, meaning that a case is sent to a juvenile court or juvenile intake agency to be examined.

> **Diversion:** An intake department takes a look at the case and comes to a decision such as dismissing, or cancelling, a case; coming to an agreement without filing charges; or filing formal charges.

> **Detention:** A youth is held behind bars while the case is being processed, before the court has heard a case.

> **Having charges filed:** If a case is going to court, this means charges have been filed. This is where a decision is made about whether the youth will be tried as a juvenile or as an adult.

> **Delinquent findings:** Being found delinquent is like being found guilty or convicted, the word used in (adult) criminal court. At this point a decision is made about punishment. Some examples include probation, being sent to a residential facility, or community service.

> **Probation:** This is when a youth's activities are monitored for a specific period of time. Getting caught

doing something wrong during probation can get a youth sent to a detention facility.

> **Being transferred to adult court:** Transfer is when a judge is asked to send a case to criminal court instead of hearing it out in juvenile court. Punishment in criminal court cases can be more serious, and if convicted, the youth is sent to regular prison instead of a juvenile detention facility.

ONE WORD: LAWYER

Solving the problem of DMC is ongoing. Although many organizations, including government offices, want to solve this problem, they have a long way to go. Black youth have the greatest disparities when it comes to sentencing of youth. They make up 26 percent of young people arrested, 44 percent of those detained, 46 percent of youth whose cases get sent to criminal court, and 58 percent of those sent to state prisons. According to the W. Haywood Burns Institute, black youth are 4.6 times as likely to be locked up compared to white youth, while Latinos are 1.8 percent as likely and American Indians 3.2 times as likely. If there is any silver lining in this, it is that the number of youth being locked up is going down for all groups.

Although many minorities face unequal treatment at the hands of the juvenile justice system, it is important to have someone who can fight for your case and get you the best possible result if you find yourself in trouble. That person is a lawyer.

Ask for a lawyer as soon as possible. You can even ask for one when police stop and detain you. As soon as you say, "I want a lawyer. I will not answer any questions without my lawyer," you do not have to answer any more of their questions until he or she arrives.

If you or your family already have a lawyer, you will be able to call him or her. If you don't have a lawyer and can't afford one, you still have a right to one if you are charged with a crime. You can apply for a lawyer through legal aid, and, if you fit the requirements, you will be assigned one. Ask for a lawyer that has experience working with juveniles. The more experience he or she has with cases like yours, the better.

A lawyer will help you with all aspects of the legal process. He or she will be there when you are asked questions by the juvenile court or juvenile intake agency. A lawyer will protect your rights and make sure you are treated fairly. He or she will also be able to tell if your rights have already been violated. If your case goes to trial, a lawyer will handle it, as well as help prepare for the trial and bring in evidence and witnesses to help the case.

If you lose the case, that doesn't mean the lawyer's work is done. He or she can help get you the best sentence possible and can help turn what could have been a jail sentence into community service or probation.

A final note about your relationship with your lawyer: you can and should tell your lawyer the entire truth about your case. Everything you tell them is "privileged," meaning that the lawyer-client relationship prevents your lawyer from telling other people information you have told him or her relating to your case, except with very limited exceptions.

If you cannot afford a lawyer, take advantage of programs that offer free legal services for youth to find a lawyer who will look out for your best interests.

TURNING IT AROUND

As discussed earlier, a drug conviction can follow you for the rest of your life. This is true for other types of convictions. Generally if you were convicted as a juvenile, your records cannot follow you for the rest of your life. However, verdicts such as adult convictions and youth offender verdicts (for those between the ages of sixteen and nineteen) are not sealed. They can in fact follow you into adulthood and be used against you if you are ever convicted in an adult court). People such as college admissions officers and potential employers can see these records. Other exceptions are that government agencies and entities will have access to these sealed records (and they can form the basis for the rejection of an application to become a police officer, government agent, or even to join the military).

It's not just the conviction that affects your future. When you come out of a juvenile detention center or a prison, you may be facing a shaky future. Perhaps your facility didn't provide you with an adequate education. You may be returning to a bad home life or a poor, high-crime neighborhood. You may not have the skills to get a job. Recidivism, or returning to a life of crime, is a big danger. So is homelessness. A study by the Wilder Research Center found that 46 percent of homeless youth between the ages of ten and seventeen had spent time in a correctional facility.

This is a crucial time to seek out help. Know that there are organizations and people out there who want to help you. Strangely, this may start at the correctional facility. Many work with youth before they are released to come up with a plan for reentering society. They can provide information on housing, education, treatment programs, and jobs.

When Julie Kisaka was fifteen years old, she took her parents' car and crashed it into their building. When her parents needed to make a report for insurance purposes, the police arrested Kisaka. The judge scheduled a hearing, but also decided to put Kisaka into detention for the thirty days before the date of the hearing. The judge thought it would teach her a lesson. According to Kisaka, what she did learn in prison instead was how to be a criminal. The detention center was a crowded place with very little structure.

Fortunately for Kisaka, those thirty days were all she would see behind bars. Kisaka received probation and, with her parents' support, managed to finish high school and college and go on to law school.

BEHIND BARS . . . OR NOT

If you are arrested, there are many points at which you can find yourself behind bars. The first may happen not long after you are arrested. While you are being held at the police station, you have a right to make a phone call. That call should be to your parent or guardian, and you should ask them to come to the station as soon as they can. If your parent or guardian comes to the station, the chances that you will be allowed to go home with them increases. If no one comes to pick you up, you may be held in detention. You may be kept behind bars or in a special home until your case is reviewed. (Even if your parent or guardian does come, there may be other factors involved that may get you placed in detention.)

It is not that simple in adult court (even for teens). If you are arrested, you must go before a court (this proceeding is called an arraignment) and in most cases the court will either set bail or release you on your own recognizance or into the custody of a parent or guardian. In some very serious cases, however, the court will not set bail and will instead determine that there are circumstances that require detention.

A police officer in Oregon is taking information from a boy he has arrested. This is a situation that could make anyone frightened and nervous.

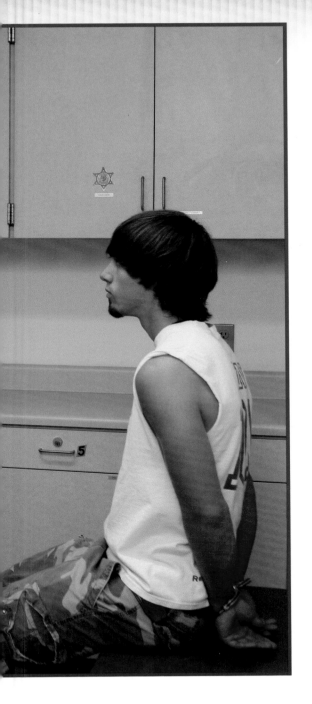

Getting arrested is naturally a stressful, unpleasant experience. It is a situation that can make anyone angry and frightened and you may want to yell or talk back to the cops. This behavior can be reported and affect you negatively when a judge is deciding whether or not you should be detained while your case gets heard. If you try to keep your emotions in check and stay calm, your chances of getting released to your parent or guardian are much better.

Having a respectful attitude can also help when your case is being examined. After your arrest, a juvenile intake office examines your case. A person from that office reads about the case and interviews you, your parents or guardian, and anyone involved in the case. They also look at your background: grades, extracurricular activities, whether you have been suspended, whether or not you were in trouble with the law before. The juvenile intake office can decide your fate. If you come across as respectful and responsible and show that you made a one-time mistake, the intake office has the power to dismiss your case, meaning they won't bring you to juvenile court, or come to a solution like probation that might not even show up on your record.

Keep in mind that the process described above applies if you are going through the juvenile court process. Unfortunately, many teens end up with their cases tried in adult court instead of juvenile court, even through the teens may not yet be legal adults. This could mean spending time in adult jail or prison, and a record that follows you when you get out.

Another option you may receive is a diversion. This will allow you to be placed in a special program that helps you deal with whatever issue got you arrested in the first place and teaches you how to stay out of trouble. In addition, diversion programs offer other services like therapy or counseling and can help you with schoolwork or getting your GED. If you go through the program and pass successfully, the charges will be dropped from your record.

Unfortunately, racial discrimination is a reality in our world. People all over the country and the world are working hard to change that, but in the meantime it's a harsh truth that you or someone you know might have to deal with it. Remember that there are some simple ways to stay out of trouble in the first place. But if you find yourself in a bind there are people out there who can help you.

You, too, can get involved and stand up for your rights. Check out organizations like United We Dream and the Black Youth Project.

GLOSSARY

adequate Enough of something, whether in number or condition.

administrator Someone responsible or involved in running an organization, like a principal or superintendent for a school.

botch To mess something up in a serious way.

delinquent Someone, usually a young person, who is apt to commit crime.

discriminatory Unfair treatment, especially toward a particular group of people or a person from a particular group.

disparity A large difference between two or more things; an inequality.

disproportionate Something out of proportion in comparison to other things; too big or small.

epidemic A disease, or something that behaves like a disease, that quickly infects a large number of people.

felony A serious crime for which the punishment is a minimum of one year in state or federal prison.

furtive Appearing sneaky or guilty; trying to avoid attention.

immigration detention center A place immigrants are sent when a decision is being made about their legal status, often after contact with police.

incarceration The act of being locked away.

influential Something or someone with the ability to cause great change.

ordeal A horrible, painful, or difficult experience.

policy A plan or set of general rules that an organization or government operates by.

possession In crime, the act of controlling or having an illegal substance.

prosecutor A lawyer who tries to prove that a person on trial is guilty.

recall To remember something, as in bringing it up from your memory.

recidivism Returning to a life of crime.

recognizance A legal obligation or promise to perform an act, such as to returning to court, without posting any bail.

relentless Something that continues at a constant pace or intensity without slowing down or letting up.

summons A ticket that requires the person receiving it to come to court

unconstitutional Something that goes against the laws in the constitution.

Center for Children's Law and Policy
1701 K Street NW, Suite 1100
Washington, DC 20006
(202) 667-0377
Website: http://www.cclp.org
The Center for Children's Law and Policy provides English
and Spanish language reports on race and juvenile
justice issues.

The Centre for Children and Families in the Justice System
254 Pall Mall Street
Suite 200
London, ON N6A 5P6
Canada
(519) 679-7250
Website: http://www.lfcc.on.ca
The Centre for Children and Families in the Justice System
advocates for children involved in the criminal justice
system. The site provides research reports and
resources for kids and families.

The Centre for Restorative Justice
School of Criminology
Saywell Hall, Room 10216
8888 University Drive
Burnaby, BC V5A 1S6
Canada
(778) 782-7627
Website: http://www.sfu.ca/restorative_justice
The Centre for Restorative Justice provides alternatives to
incarceration.

Coalition for Juvenile Justice
1319 F Street NW, Suite 402
Washington, DC 20004
(202) 467-0864
Website: http://www.juvjustice.org
The Coalition for Juvenile Justice is a network of state
    groups that works to prevent children from getting
    caught in the system and helps them when they are.

Juvenile Law Center
The Philadelphia Building
1315 Walnut Street, 4th Floor
Philadelphia, PA 19107
(215) 625-0551
Website: http://www.jlc.org
The Juvenile Law Center advocates for children caught up
    in the juvenile justice system. The center also runs a
    program that allows young people to come together
    as advocates and offer solutions to fix the system.

National Council of La Raza
1126 16th Street NW, Suite 600
Washington, DC 20036
(202) 785-1670
Website: http://www.nclr.org
The National Council of La Raza focuses on fighting for the
    rights of Hispanic Americans.

The Osborne Association
175 Remsen Street, No. 8
Brooklyn, NY 11201

55

(718) 637-6560
Website: http://www.osborneny.org
The Osborne Association provides educational prepara-
tion, career training, and wellness services to those
who have been to jail.

Race Forward
900 Alice Street, Suite 400
Oakland, CA 94607
(510) 653-3415
Website: http://www.raceforward.org
Race Forward advocates for racial justice through research;
its new site, Colorlines; and leadership training.

WEBSITES

Because of the changing nature of Internet links, Rosen
Publishing has developed an online list of websites related
to the subject of this book. This site is updated regularly.
Please use this link to access this list:

http://www.rosenlinks.com/KYR/Race

FOR FURTHER READING

Abrams, Laura S., and Ben Anderson-Nathe. *Compassionate Confinement: A Year in the Life of Unit C.* New Brunswick, NJ: Rutgers University Press, 2012.

Alexander, Michelle. *The New Jim Crow: Mass Incarceration in the Age of Colorblindness.* New York, NY: Kaplan, 2012.

Alexie, Sherman. *The Absolutely True Diary of a Part-Time Indian.* New York, NY: Little, Brown & Company, 2007.

Barrett, Carla J. *Courting Kids: Inside an Experimental Youth Court.* New York, NY: NYU Press, 2013.

Bates, Krisin A., and Richelle S. Swan. *Juvenile Delinquency in a Diverse Society.* Los Angeles, CA: SAGE 2014.

Bernstein, Nell. *Burning Down the House: The End of Juvenile Prison.* New York, NY: New Press, 2014.

Chomsky, Aviva. *Undocumented: How Immigration Became Illegal.* Boston, Mass: Beacon Press, 2014.

Coe, Booth. *Bronxwood.* New York, NY: Scholastic, 2011.

Hancock, Ange-Marie. *Solidarity Politics for Millenials: A Guide to Ending the Oppression Olympics.* New York, NY: Palgrave Macmillan, 2011.

Jones, Sabrina, and Marc Mauer. *Race to Incarcerate: A Graphic Retelling.* New York, NY: New Press, 2013.

Kennedy, David M. *Don't Shoot: One Man, a Street Fellowship and the End of Violence in Inner-City America.* New York, NY: Bloomsbury, 2011.

Laura, Crystal T. Being Bad: *My Baby Brother and the School-to-Prison Pipeline.* New York, NY: Teachers College Press, 2014.

Myers, Walter Dean. *Lockdown.* New York, NY: Amistad, 2010.

O'Shea, Marie Glancy, Laura Longhine, and Keith Hefner. *Growing Up Muslim in America: Stories by Muslim Youth.* New York, NY: New York Youth Communication Center, 2010.

Rios, Victor M. *Punished: Policing the Lives of Black and Latino Boys.* New York, NY: NYU Press, 2011.

Sullivan, Irene. *Raised by the Courts: One Judge's Insight Into Juvenile Justice.* New York, NY: 2010.

Tilton, Jennifer. *Dangerous or Endangered? Race and the Politics of Youth in Urban America.* New York, NY: New York University Press, 2010.

Townsend, Trinity and Travis. *The Stop and Frisk Handbook.* Brooklyn, NY: The Optimum Institute of Empowerment, 2012.

Walker, Samuel, Cassia Spohn, and Miriam DeLone. *The Color of Justice: Race, Ethnicity, and Crisis in America.* Belmont, CA: Wordsworth, 2012.

Weissman, Marsha. *Prelude to Prison: Student Perspectives on School Suspension.* Syracuse, NY: Syracuse University Press, 2014.

BIBLIOGRAPHY

Bunting, Will, Ezekiel Edwards, and Lynda Garcia. *The War on Marijuana in Black and White.* American Civil Liberties Union. June 2013.

Center for Constitutional Rights. "Floyd, et al. v. City of New York, et al." Retrieved September 20, 2014 (http://ccrjustice.org/stopandfrisk#weaponsyield).

Drug Policy Alliance. "The Drug War, Mass Incarceration and Race." January 2014 . Retrieved February 12, 2015 (http://www.drugpolicyorg/resource/drug -war-mass-incarceration-and-race).

Ella Baker Center for Human Rights. "Know Your Rights." Retrieved September 4, 2014 (http://ellabakercenter .org/know-your-rights).

Fellner, Jamie. "Punishment and Prejudice: Racial Disparities in the War on Drugs." *Human Rights Watch*, Vol. 12, No 2., May 2000.

Ferrer, Carmel. "Where Zero Tolerance Makes Zero Sense." ACLU Blog of Rights, May 1, 2014. Retrieved October 14, 2014 (https://www.aclu.org/blog/racial-justice/ where-zero-tolerance-makes-zero-sense).

Jones, Jessica. "N.C. Sheriff Terry Johnson On Trial For Racial Profiling." NPR, August 15, 2014. Retrieved October 14, 2014 (http://www.npr.org/2014/08 /15/340562910/n-c-sheriff-terry-johnson-on-trial -for-racial-profiling).

Kansal, Tushar. *Racial Disparity in Sentencing: A Review of the Literature.* The Sentencing Project, January 2005.

Leadership Conference on Civil Rights Education Fund. "Wrong Then, Wrong Now: Racial Profiling Before and After September 11, 2001." 2001.

McCalmont, Lucy. "Eric Holder Recalls Being Hassled by Cops." Politico, August 20, 2014 . Retrieved February 12, 2015 (http://www.politico.com/story/2014/08/eric-holder-in-ferguson-we-can-make-it-better-110196.html?hp=t2_3).

New York Civil Liberties Union. "Stop-and-Frisk Data." Retrieved September 4, 2014 (http://www.nyclu.org/content/stop-and-frisk-data).

Roberts, Sam. "Author of 'Broken Windows' Policing Defends His Theory." New York Times, August 10, 2014. Retrieved October 14, 2014 (http://www.nytimes.com/2014/08/11/nyregion/author-of-broken-windows-policing-defends-his-theory.html?_r=0).

Rovner, Joshua. "Disproportionate Minority Contact." The Sentencing Project, May 2014.

Shelden, Randall. "Race and the Drug War." Center on Juvenile and Criminal Justice, June 8, 2013. Retrieved October 14, 2014 (http://www.cjcj.org/news/6226).

Szalavitz, Maia. "Study: Whites More Likely to Abuse Drugs Than Blacks." Time, November 7, 2011. Retrieved September 4, 2014 (http://healthland.time.com/2011/11/07/study-whites-more-likely-to-abuse-drugs-than-blacks)

U.S. Department of Education Office for Civil Rights. Civil Rights Data Collection. "Data Snapshot: School Discipline." March 21, 2014.

Warikoo, Niraj. "Ohio Woman Sues FBI, Airline for Racial Profiling." USA Today, January 22, 2013. Retrieved September 4, 2014 (http://www.usatoday.com/story/

news/nation/2013/01/22/racial-profiling-lawsuit/
1856619).

Wilmot, Kiera. "An Unexpected Reaction: Why a Science
Experiment Gone Bad Doesn't Make Me a Criminal."
ACLU Blog of Rights, May 23, 2013. Retrieved
September 4, 2014 (https://www.aclu.org/blog/
racial-justice/unexpected-reaction-why-science
-experiment-gone-bad-doesnt-make-me-criminal).

Yu, Elly. "Life after Juvenile Detention." Juvenile Justice
Information Exchange, May 23, 2014. Retrieved
September 4, 2014 (http://jjie.org/life-after-juvenile
-detention).

Zamani, Nahal, et al. "Stop and Frisk: The Human Impact."
Center for Constitutional Rights, July 2012.

INDEX

ABOUT THE AUTHOR

Corinne Grinapol is a writer living in Brooklyn, New York. As a former fact-checker, she enjoys deep dives into primary documents and research reports, which she uses in her research for all her books.

ABOUT THE EXPERT REVIEWER

Lindsay A. Lewis, Esq., is a practicing criminal defense attorney in New York City, where she handles a wide range of matters, from those discussed in this series to high-profile federal criminal cases. She believes that each and every defendant deserves a vigorous and informed defense. Ms. Lewis is a graduate of the Benjamin N. Cardozo School of Law and Vassar College.

PHOTO CREDITS